WALKER'S FRIEND

A MISCELLANY OF WIT AND WISDOM

JUDE PALMER

THE WALKER'S FRIEND

With research by Jennifer Barclay

Illustrations by Kath Walker

Summersdale Publishers Ltd
46 West Street
Chichester
West Sussex
PO19 1RP
UK

www.summersdale.com

Printed and bound in Great Britain

ISBN: 978-1-84953-052-1

Substantial discounts on bulk quantities of Summersdale books are available to corporations, professional associations and other organisations. For details contact Summersdale Publishers by telephone: +44 (0) 1243 771107, fax: +44 (0) 1243 786300 or email: nicky@summersdale.com.

THE
WALKER'S
FRIEND

A MISCELLANY OF
WIT AND WISDOM

JUDE PALMER

CONTENTS

INTRODUCTION

It's simply a matter of putting on your old boots, hoisting your pack and heading off down that winding path.

GILLIAN SOUTER, *SLOW JOURNEYS*

Walking is currently one of the most popular recreations in the world, at least among those of us who sit at desks staring at computers for most of our day, and it stands to reason. No matter your age or income level, you have everything to gain from going out for a walk, including a clear head, a healthier body and a warmer heart; nothing to fear except the weather, nothing to lose except your will to go back to work. Luckily, we have plenty of space in which to do it. There are 113,000 national parks around the world, occupying 12.9 per cent of the Earth's land mass, which is 18 times larger than the combined urban landscapes of the planet. If that's not encouraging, I don't know what is.

A walk may permit you to see your own town or neighbourhood differently, or it may take you halfway around the world. Robert Louis Stevenson wrote about the 'jolly humours' to be gained from walking, including 'the hope and spirit with which the march begins at morning, and the peace and spiritual repletion of the evening's rest'. This was certainly true for the composer Felix Mendelssohn who, when grieving the death of his sister in 1847, could only calm his mind with long walks.

Rambling feet and rambling thoughts go well together. This miscellany, for anyone who has ever enjoyed walking at any level, is filled with inspiring and amusing quotations from across the centuries, with trivia and practical information on the wealth of wildlife and the foraging possibilities to be found in the countryside. Wherever you are, this book is intended to remind you of the myriad pleasures of walking.

Give me my scallop-shell of quiet,
My staff of faith to walk upon,
My scrip of joy, immortal diet,
My bottle of salvation,
My gown of glory, hope's true gage,
And thus I'll take my pilgrimage.

SIR WALTER RALEIGH, 'THE PASSIONATE MAN'S PILGRIMAGE'

FOOTLOOSE AND FANCY FREE

*Walking can in the end become an addiction...
a delectable madness, very good for sanity.*

COLIN FLETCHER

TO WALK MAY BE TO...

... ramble, roam, ambulate, strike out, travel, stroll, traipse, gallivant...

A WALKER MAY BE A...

... journeyer, trekker, tourer, excursionist, explorer, pathfinder, adventurer, mover, gadabout, itinerant, peregrinator, drifter, floater, wandering scholar, vagabond, vagrant, hobo, landloper, swagman, nomad, migrant, foot passenger, hoofer, footbacker, trailsman, tramper, marcher, foot soldier, paddlefoot, hitchhiker, wanderer, wayfarer, rover...

I have walked myself into my best thoughts.

Søren Kierkegaard

When Tess and I walked Britain's coast, I discovered a deep contentment brought on by the world close by and the simplicity of life on the road; where so many daily trappings are shed and the air that you breathe and the ground which you tread become important.

Spud Talbot-Ponsonby,
WHO WALKED AROUND THE COAST OF BRITAIN WITH HER DOG

I like the steady rhythm that enables me to forget my feet and concentrate on sights, sounds and thoughts.

BERNARD LEVIN, *FROM THE CAMARGUE TO THE ALPS*

*Few men know how to take a walk. The
qualifications... are endurance, plain clothes,
old shoes, an eye for nature, good humour,
vast curiosity, good speech, good silence
and nothing too much.*

RALPH WALDO EMERSON

*Whereas jets and the Internet collapse the
planet, walking expands it and returns to
the walker a sense of its proportions and the
intimacy of its appeal to the senses.*

CHARLES WILKINS, *WALK TO NEW YORK*

A SPRING IN MY STEP

Daffy Down Dilly
Has come to town
With a yellow petticoat
And a green gown

FOLK SAYING

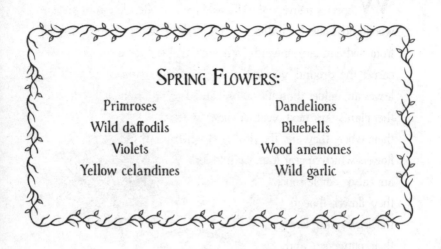

SPRING FLOWERS:

Primroses

Wild daffodils

Violets

Yellow celandines

Dandelions

Bluebells

Wood anemones

Wild garlic

*I never saw daffodils so beautiful. They grew
among the mossy stones about and about them,
some rested their heads upon these stones as on
a pillow for weariness and the rest tossed and
reeled and danced and seemed as if they
verily laughed with the wind that
blew upon them over the lake.*

DOROTHY WORDSWORTH

Wild garlic, or ramsons, is one of the first signs of spring. A species native to the UK, wild garlic is often found in ancient woodland. Look for brilliant green blades poking through the soil from mid-January onwards. Wherever its long, spear-shaped leaves carpet the ground, you will notice a strong, garlicky aroma. The leaves are milder than the bulbs – and digging up the bulbs depletes the plants for next year, so best to leave them where they are. The clusters of white flowers which appear from April to June are also edible once they flower, though the leaves can lose their pungency and become tougher.

Garlic contains allicin, thought to be anti-fungal and anti-bacterial; other properties in it aid circulation and keep the cardiovascular systems functioning efficiently. Add chopped wild garlic to a salad or soup, omelette or pasta sauce – or brush olive oil on bread, toast it on either side, then sprinkle with finely chopped garlic leaves, sea salt and pepper.

Wild garlic

Whan that Aprille with his shoures sote
The droghte of Marche hath perced to the rote,
And bathed every veyne in swich licour,
Of which vertu engendred is the flour;
Whan Zephirus eek with his swete breeth
Inspired hath in every holt and heath
The tender croppes, and the yonge sonne
Hath in the Ram his halfe cours y-ronne,
And smale fowles maken melodye,
That slepen al the night with open yë,
(So priketh hem nature in hir corages):
Than longen folk to goon on pilgrimages

HENRY CHAUCER, *THE CANTERBURY TALES*

Early spring brings buds and birds to the trees and lambs to the fields, but also 'spring bloom' to the sea. As winter has churned the sand and silt into welcome nutrients, with the coming sunshine this becomes a rich food supply for plankton, microscopic plants and animals, which gives off a sparkling luminescence at night. If you find yourself walking near the Menai Straits in Wales, try to get a bottle and see how it lights up. The sea will also look greener and less clear. The plankton in turn becomes an essential food source for fish such as mackerel and herring, which migrate in spring to shallower coastal waters. So spring is also a great time to eat fresh local fish.

The cowslip is a member of the primrose family, and blooms in April and May with yellow flowers smaller than the primrose and up to 30 cm off the ground. It likes sunny, well-drained meadows. The name derives from Old English 'cuslyppe', meaning cow dung – cowslips flourish among cowpats. Another colourful member of the family is the Scarlet Pimpernel, with scarlet or pink blooms (though occasionally blue) of five round petals. These are found near cultivated land or sand dunes in the summer.

Oh, to be in England
Now that April's there,
And whoever wakes in England
Sees, some morning, unaware,
That the lowest boughs and the brushwood sheaf
Round the elm-tree bole are in tiny leaf,
While the chaffinch sings on the orchard bough
In England—now!

And after April, when May follows,
And the whitethroat builds, and all the swallows!
Hark, where my blossomed pear-tree in the hedge
Leans to the field and scatters on the clover
Blossoms and dewdrops—at the bent spray's edge—
That's the wise thrush; he sings each song twice over,
Lest you should think he never could recapture
The first fine careless rapture!
And though the fields look rough with hoary dew,
All will be gay when noontide wakes anew
The buttercups, the little children's dower
—Far brighter than this gaudy melon-flower!

ROBERT BROWNING, 'HOME THOUGHTS FROM ABROAD'

AND DID THOSE FEET IN ANCIENT TIMES

Let the road rise to meet you.

IRISH TRADITIONAL TRAVELLER'S BLESSING

ANCIENT HISTORY

The Ridgeway, called the oldest road in Europe, has been in continuous use for at least 5,000 years and is now a British national trail stretching for 85 miles from Wessex to the Chilterns, passing Neolithic and Bronze Age burial mounds and Iron Age hill forts.

Many of Britain's local paths were probably created by the Anglo-Saxons who came from northern Germany and around the Baltic to settle in Britain after the Romans left.

Medieval drovers created many of our ancient footpaths, taking animals to market. A drover's track under Kinder Scout still has a wayside water trough, and one in Angus has a tethering ring. Wayside inns would have been used by these men, where they would have soaped the soles of their stockings against blisters and wore brown paper next to their skin, before covering twenty miles a day with their flocks and herds. To protect the livestock's feet, they tarred the feet of geese, put pigs in leather galoshes, and nailed iron shoes to hooves of cattle.

For others in the Middle Ages, going on a pilgrimage was often the only way to travel and see the world. Your masters would always give you permission to set out on a pilgrimage, and no matter how poor you were, you could beg for food and shelter.

HISTORICAL FACTS

218 BC: Carthaginian general Hannibal led soldiers and elephants in a march from Carthage across the Alps.

AD 100: Emperor Hadrian toured his whole empire on foot.

1589: Sir Robert Carey walked 300 miles from London to Berwick for a bet.

1802: William Wordsworth completes an ascent of Broad Stand on Scafell Pike during a 100-mile walking tour.

1824: Association for the Protection of Ancient Footpaths around York founded to reassert the rights of the poor against wealthy landowners and their gamekeepers.

1864: The Black Forest Wanderverein or walking club was formed.

1871: John and Paul Naylor walk from Land's End to John O'Groats.

1932: Mass Trespass of Kinder Scout in the Peak District by 400 ramblers demanding access led to five ringleaders receiving a total of 17 months imprisonment.

1948: Earl Victor Shaffer became the first person to hike the complete Appalachian Trail.

RECENT CENTURIES

A wood or cast-iron post with one or more fingers pointing in different directions to different places, with the respective distances given, is known in Britain and Ireland as a fingerpost or guide post.

The oldest fingerpost is thought to be that close to Chipping Campden in Gloucestershire, dated 1669 and pointing to Oxford, Warwick, Gloucester and Worcester (abbreviated to 'Gloster' and 'Woster').

The Highways Act 1766 and Turnpike Roads Act 1773 made their use on turnpike roads compulsory. Road signposts were removed during World War Two, lest enemy forces use them for navigation, and only replaced in the late 1940s.

In the 1960s new regulations encouraged authorities to replace traditional fingerposts with the new designs, but many traditional and historic ones survived, especially in rural areas, and now regulations encourage their maintenance.

Once trodden by human feet, a natural path becomes a work of man, each traveller marking the way for the next.

J. R. L. ANDERSON AND FAY GODWIN, *THE OLDEST ROAD, AN EXPLORATION OF THE RIDGEWAY*

Walking became a popular sport in the eighteenth and nineteenth centuries, one of its most famous proponents being 'The Celebrated Pedestrian' Captain Robert Barclay Allardice, who walked a thousand miles in as many hours, while the botanical society at Eccles in Lancashire was rambling 30–40 miles on Sundays as early as 1777.

The first Enclosure Acts in England in the eighteenth and nineteenth centuries divided up the open fields, and roughly 200,000 miles of mostly very straight hedgerow were planted at that time. But this caused common land to become inaccessible to walkers, temporarily dispatching with the long-established rights of way.

The world's first official national park was Yellowstone, established in the US in 1872. Forty years earlier, four pieces of land around Hot Springs in Arkansas had been set aside by then President Andrew Jackson.

In 1935 the Ramblers Association was founded to create national parks, protect rights of way and maintain access to mountains and moorland. The Peak District became the first national park in Britain in 1951, followed in the same year by the Lake District, Snowdonia and Dartmoor. The Act of Parliament that made them possible was passed in 1949; Lewis Silkin, the Minister for Town and Country Planning, called it 'the most exciting act of the postwar parliament'.

*It is customary for these walkers,
as they are called, to enter a house
without knocking, and take a seat
by the fire... Some still retain the
good custom of keeping a
bed for the walker.*

DENHAM, *POPULAR RHYMES*

FAMOUS WALKER: LAURIE LEE

author of *As I Walked Out One Midsummer Morning*

In 1934, at the age of twenty, Lee walked from Gloucestershire to London, to earn a living playing the violin and labouring on building sites. He set out carrying a small tent, his violin wrapped in a blanket, a change of clothes, a tin of treacle biscuits, and some cheese, taking a circuitous route so that he could see 'the real sea' for the first time, and busking his way along the south coast. Tall, slim, blond and charming, he possessed an attractive sense of fun in spite of a struggle against illness and depression.

In 1936 he left England by boat and walked across Spain from Vigo to Granada just before the outbreak of the Civil War (1936–39), spending the winter in Almunecar. Then, a year later, after spells in Reading and Montpellier, he undertook a walk over the Pyrenees into Spain again to fight in the Republican International Brigades.

On his return, he worked as a journalist and scriptwriter, making documentaries during World War Two. It wasn't until thirty years later that he transformed his travel experience into books: *As I Walked Out One Midsummer Morning*, which describes the walk across Spain, was published in 1969, ten years after his first autobiographical novel *Cider With Rosie*, which began as sketches of his childhood published in magazines and went on to sell more than six million copies, and twenty years before the final work, *A Moment of War*.

Lee thought of himself primarily as a poet, though he also wrote travel books, essays, a radio play and short stories. In his last years he spent his time either in his corner of the Chelsea Arts Club or the Woolpack at Slad. He died in May 1997.

IF YOU GO DOWN
TO THE WOODS TODAY

*There is a serene and settled majesty to
woodland scenery that enters into the soul
and delights and elevates it, and fills
it with noble inclinations.*

WASHINGTON IRVING

Leaves are verbs that conjugate the seasons.

GRETEL EHRLICH

According to folklore in Somerset, travellers were best to avoid entering an alder copse after dark, or they might never return. In Ireland, however, alder wood was held to be protective and used to make milking pails as it would guard the milk. It was imbued with magical qualities for resisting damp – the piles of the Rialto in Venice are alder – and its leaves in spring were sticky and therefore useful to strew over floors to catch insects.

MIRACLE TREES OF AFRICA

The Wonderboom Nature Reserve in the Magaliesberg Mountains, Pretoria, South Africa, has a wild willowleaf fig tree that is more than a thousand years old. It has three trunks and covers an area of 50 metres. Its name means 'miracle tree' in Afrikaans.

The famous Baobab is known as the 'upside-down tree' because of its shape; an Arabic legend says that it was the devil who pulled out the tree and planted it upside down, while an older African myth claims that it was the hyena who did so, shortly after creation.

The Tree of Ténéré, an acacia, was once the most isolated tree on earth, a landmark on caravan routes through the Sahara in north-east Niger. Surviving from the days when the desert was less dry, its nearest neighbour was 120 miles (200 kilometres) away. It was knocked down in 1973, allegedly by a drunken (and/or extremely unlucky) truck driver.

The tree which moves some to tears of joy is in the eyes of others only a green thing that stands in the way.

WILLIAM BLAKE, *The Letters*

Two hikers on a forest trail in Canada came around the bend to find an enormous bear a hundred yards ahead. The bear has spotted them, makes aggressive noises and starts making its way towards them fast. The first hiker puts down his backpack and removes a pair of running shoes, takes off his boots, and starts lacing up the runners. His friend is horrified. 'Are you crazy?! You'll never outrun a bear!' The first hiker replies 'I don't have to outrun the bear...'

Nature's peace will flow into you as sunshine flows into trees. The winds will blow their freshness into you, and the storms their energy, while cares will drop off like falling leaves.

JOHN MUIR

HOW TO IDENTIFY TYPES OF DEER WHEN WALKING IN THE WOODS:

Red deer – red-brown coats in summer, dark brown in winter, and the tallest at up to 1.3 m with large antlers (males).

Sika deer – also red-brown but with white spots in summer, darker colour in winter, and a white rump; not so tall, medium-sized antlers.

Roe deer – red-brown in summer but greyish in winter, shorter again, and with black markings either side of the nose and short antlers.

Fallow deer – fawn in colour, with white speckles on the back, tall with large antlers.

Reeves' muntjac – much smaller, light brown; originally from China, they escaped from Woburn Park and are now found in south and central England.

Chinese water deer – escaped from Whipsnade Zoo, now found in central England; light in summer and grey-brown in winter, just bigger than the muntjac, with no antlers and big black eyes and nose, and occasionally tusks.

Deer tracks

Being thus prepared for us in all ways, and made beautiful, and good for food, and for building, and for instruments of our hands, this race of plants, deserving boundless affection and admiration from us, becomes, in proportion to their obtaining it, a nearly perfect test of our being in right temper of mind and way of life; so that no one can be far wrong in either who loves trees enough...

JOHN RUSKIN, *MODERN PAINTERS VI*

In days gone by, a lost traveller would seek shelter under the holy beech tree to be safe, as his prayers would then go straight to heaven. The bark of the beech is deadly to snakes, and a tea made with pigs' lard was said to alleviate rheumatism.

The beech tree has a smooth grey bark, and its oval leaves (a rich chestnut colour when dry in winter) are pointed at the top.

I frequently tramped eight or ten miles through the deepest snow to keep an appointment with a beech-tree, or a yellow birch, or an old acquaintance among the pines.

HENRY DAVID THOREAU

WALK AND BE HEALTHY

The sum of the whole is this: walk and be happy, walk and be healthy... The wandering man knows of certain ancients, far gone in years, who have staved off infirmities and dissolution by earnest walking – hale fellows close upon eighty and ninety, but brisk as boys.

CHARLES DICKENS

The US National Institution for Mental Health and researchers from the University of Kansas found that regular walkers were better able to cope with stressful life changes, and 30 minutes of vigorous exercise and a change of environment had a significant impact on anger management methods.

Glasgow University research for the British Heart Foundation shows that while an after-dinner walk can aid digestion, the health benefits of walking before a rich meal are more effective and long-lasting.

Walking will also boost your sex life, according to reports from the University of California, San Diego. Studies on men who took part in moderate exercise including walking at a hearty pace three to four days a week found that subjects reported that their sex life was more satisfying.

Exeter University experts established that taking a 15-minute stroll significantly lowered the cravings for chocolate among those with a sweet tooth. They also discovered that going for a one-mile walk when a nicotine craving kicked in reduced the desire to smoke for around 84 minutes, more than three times the usual.

Lack of activity destroys the good condition of every human being, while movement and methodical physical exercise save it and preserve it.

PLATO

Biomechanically and physiologically, walking as often as you can is among the best forms of activity to improve fitness and health.

JOHN BREWER, PROFESSOR OF SPORT,
UNIVERSITY OF BEDFORDSHIRE

Steve Vaught, known as 'Fat Man Walking', began a walk across the United States from Oceanside, California on 10 April 2005, weighing around 410 pounds, and ended in New York City on 9 May 2006. His goal was to lose weight and regain his life, walking through Arizona, New Mexico, Texas, Oklahoma, Missouri, Illinois, Indiana, Ohio, Pennsylvania and New Jersey, and mostly camping at night, carrying his own food and water. From being so overweight that he could 'hardly walk through a store', his physical condition gradually improved until he was averaging 15 miles a day and in a year lost 114 pounds. Appearing on *The Today Show* in the US, he said: 'I think everybody needs to take a long walk sometimes.' He was impressed by the kindness of strangers and learned to live in the present.

WWW.THEFATMANWALKING.COM

THE HEALTH BENEFITS OF WALKING

AFTER 1–5 MINUTES:

Setting out begins production of energy creating chemicals and raises your heartbeat to around 100 beats per minute.

AFTER 6–10 MINUTES:

As your breathing and pulse rate increase, your body starts to extract fuel in the form of glucose from carbohydrates and fat stores. Your adrenal glands release chemicals to expand your blood vessels to bring extra blood and oxygen to muscles.

AFTER 10–15 MINUTES:

As your body warms up, any aches or tightness in joints fades. Your body will start burning up to five calories per minute (five times more than at rest).

AFTER 15–20 MINUTES:

Your heartbeat will be 100–140 beats per minute (take your pulse for ten seconds and multiply by six to check). You'll be burning 6–8 calories a minute and hormones release fuel to the muscles.

AFTER 20–40 MINUTES:

Muscle tension has been eased and you're getting a natural high from endorphins and other feel-good chemicals.

AFTER 40–60 MINUTES:

Your muscles may feel a little fatigued as your carbohydrate stores are depleted, and your metabolism starts to burn fat for energy. You're burning fewer calories than at the 20-minute point, but still more than when you started, and the calorie burn will remain elevated for several hours after your walk.

ADAPTED FROM *COUNTRY WALKING* MAGAZINE

Walking is the best possible exercise.
Habituate yourself to walk very far.

THOMAS JEFFERSON

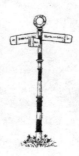

If there was a pill that could lower the risk of
chronic disease like walking does then
people would be clamouring for it.

JOANN MANSON, PROFESSOR, HARVARD UNIVERSITY

A Mind for Higher Things

*Great things are done when
men and mountains meet.*

WILLIAM BLAKE

HIGHEST POINTS IN THE UK:

Scotland: Ben Nevis – 1,344 metres
Wales: Snowdon – 1,085 metres
England: Scafell Pike – 978 metres
Northern Ireland: Slieve Donard – 850 metres

Alas, that the longest hill
Must end in a vale; but still,
Who climbs with toil, whereso'er
Shall find wings waiting there.

HENRY CHARLES BEECHING, 'GOING DOWN HILL ON A BICYLE'

MEET THE MUNROS

Scotland's highest mountains include its 283 Munros (over 3,000 feet or 914 metres). Munros are named after Sir Hugh Munro (1856–1919), who first catalogued them in *Munro's Tables* in 1891. Thereafter, if one wanted to while away the cold nights, one could still debate whether something was merely a 'Munro top', not a separate mountain. The tables continue to be revised.

What is clear is that in winter the weather conditions, including fog, wind and extreme cold, create some of the most challenging climbing in Europe. Fatalities are recorded every year.

A Munroist is a walker who has 'bagged' all the peaks. In 2009, there were 4,000 Munroists. The first 'compleationist', the Reverend A. E. Robertson, had his 1901 claim questioned, so the honour went to Ronald Burn in 1923. The average time taken to bag all Munros is eight years.

LITTLE ENGLAND

After Scafell Pike in the Lake District, the highest points in the English hill ranges are Cross Fell in the Pennines at 893 metres, Black Mountain at 703 metres, and High Willhays of Dartmoor at 621 metres. The highest points of the South Downs and North Downs are Butser Hill and Botley Hill at 270 and 268 metres respectively. The highest points in London range from Highgate Hill at 100 metres to Westerham Heights in Bromley at 245 metres.

IT'S ALL DOWNHILL FROM HERE

Walking uphill is tough, but the descent can be tricky too. Good posture is key: leaning back will send you off balance, so stay upright or lean slightly forward, keeping your weight over your hips and knees which should be slightly bent. Control your speed by shortening your stride, which will tend to lengthen automatically when moving downhill. A zig-zag route will give you better control and reduce the impact on joints.

LEDGES ON BRITISH MOUNTAINS:

Purple saxifrage

Mossy saxifrage

Moss campion

Rock speedwell

Mountain avens

Purple saxifrage

CHALK FIGURES

Figures were first cut into the chalk hillsides in southern England by pagan Celts, around 500 BC. Many have been altered over the centuries, but they remain striking features of the hills, seen from far away;

Cerne Abbas Giant, Dorchester, Dorset
Long Man of Wilmington, Windover Hill, East Sussex (226 feet high)
Bedlow and Whiteleaf Crosses, Chiltern Hills
White Horse, Uffington, Berkshire (130 feet high, 374 feet long)
White Horse, Westbury, Wiltshire
Great Red Horse, Sun Rising Hill, Tysoe, Warwickshire

Is there a felicity in the world superior to this?

JANE AUSTEN, ON WALKING IN THE HIGH DOWNS

In October 2009, Sail Chapman, aged five years, three weeks and one day, became the youngest person to walk all 214 peaks in Alfred Wainwright's Lake District guide books. He began walking the Cumbrian fells aged two with his parents and two older brothers.

You stand there as it were upon the summit of a lonely pedestal, with nothing but a rocky edge around you.

HILAIRE BELLOC, *THE HILLS AND THE SEA*

A surprising sign on the summit of the Old Man of Coniston in the Lake District looks at first sight like the triangular road warning sign advising road-users to watch out for elderly people. Look again: this one, created by artist Steve Messam, shows a couple hiking up a hill with walking poles, with the wording 'Not just elderly people'.

In his acclaimed book *Mountains of the Mind*, Robert Macfarlane explains that only three hundred years ago, the idea of endangering your life to climb a mountain 'would have been considered tantamount to lunacy'; mountains in the seventeenth century were thought of as deserts, and 'castigated as "boils" on the earth's complexion'.

And finally we were at the top, looking out across the bare peaks that gave way to green forest sweeping down to the valleys. Sheer rock steeples reached finger-like into the sky around us. The only sound was the wind that blew clouds of mist across the cliffs, covering then revealing the scenes below.

JENNIFER BARCLAY, *MEETING MR KIM*

Famous Walker: Alfred Wainwright

fell-walker and author of the *Pictorial Guide to the Lakeland Fells*

Alfred Wainwright (1907–1991) was born in Blackburn, Lancashire, and published his now famous *Pictorial Guide to the Lakeland Fells* between 1955 and 1966. All seven volumes were written and drawn by hand, with Wainwright completing one page per evening. He originally published them privately rather than search for a publisher. They were eventually taken over by the local newspaper in Kendal and were only taken on by a major publisher in the 1990s. Growing up in a poor family, as a child he walked up to 20 miles at a time and produced maps of his local area. Aged 23, he saved up enough money from his job as an accountant for the Blackburn Borough Council for a week's walking in the Lake District with his cousin, and saw his first view of the Lakeland fells in Windermere, which marked the start of his love affair with the Lake District. In 1941 he took a lesser-paying job in order to move closer to the fells. His second wife Betty McNally became his walking companion after retirement and eventually carried his ashes to Innominate Tarn at the top of Haystacks. Walkers can visit his memorial in the church at Buttermere.

His other works include the *Pennine Way Companion*, a guidebook to Britain's first long-distance path, though he never walked the entire 270-mile route in one outing. He also devised the 192-mile east-west Coast to Coast Walk, which he said 'puts the Pennine Way to shame' for its beauty, variety and interest, passing through the Lake District, Yorkshire Dales and North York Moors national parks. Many of his walks have been televised, including a BBC series presented by Julia Bradbury. An English hero, his guides to the fells have given inspiration to fell-walkers for decades.

FOOD AND DRINK

Hampstead Heath is my favourite place to walk in London. You're never more than 20 minutes from a really good pub...

JOHNNY BORRELL, SINGER, IN *THE TIMES*

KENDAL MINT CAKE

This popular climber's and walker's staple food was reputedly discovered accidentally by Joseph Wiper during his quest to make a clear glacier mint: the confectioner took his eye off the cooking pan for a minute and, resuming his task, noticed that the mixture had started to 'grain' and become cloudy. Joseph Wiper started closely-guarded production at his tiny Ferney Green factory in Kendal in 1869.

The Kendal mint cake was primarily sold to the locals at first then sent by rail to other parts in the north-east of England. In 1910 Mr Wiper retired to live in Victoria, British Columbia where one of his sons opened a shop selling Wiper's mint cake. The Kendal Mint Cake business was left to his great nephew Mr Robert Wiper, who realised its potential as an energy food and supplied Ernest Shackleton's 1914-1917 transarctic expedition and the first Everest expedition, giving mint cake a whole new image.

In 1918, Sam T. Clarke of Romney Road was invalided out of World War One and started out as a sweet wholesaler. Unable to obtain supplies of Kendal mint cake during the summer season, he purchased an old recipe and started manufacturing. The business, known as Romney's, proved quite successful, but was given a tremendous boost when, after advertising in a climbing magazine, Mr Clarke was approached by the 1953 expedition to Everest to see whether he could supply mint cake to them within seven days. Sir Edmund Hilary and Sirdar Tensing ate this mint cake on top of

Everest on 29 May 1953; Tensing also left some to appease his gods.

Mint cake is made from sugar, glucose and water in traditional copper pans on gas boilers. After cooling for several minutes, oil of peppermint is added.

CALORIC EXPENDITURES PER MILE BY WALKING

The number of calories you can burn by walking depends on your body weight and the speed of walking. For example, the average man weighs 86 kg or 191 lb. Walking at three miles per hour on a level surface will burn approximately 100 calories. The average female weighs 74 kg or 164 lb. Walking at three miles per hour on a level surface will burn just under 90 calories. Walking at two miles per hour or four miles per hour will burn a few more calories, so speed is not important, while calories burned walking at three miles per hour nearly doubles with a ten per cent incline.

For William Wordsworth, according to Thomas De Quincey, walking 'stood in the stead of wine, spirits and all other stimulants whatsoever to the animal spirits; to which, indeed, he was indebted for a life of unclouded happiness, and we for much of what is most excellent in his writings.'

An obsession among the chattering classes in the late eighteenth century was gambling, and in the 1760s John Montagu, the fourth Earl of Sandwich, created the perfect light meal for someone who didn't want to risk his night's betting by leaving the table, or get his hands greasy by touching meat – thinly sliced beef, veal or ham between thin bread and butter – 'a fact that remains debatable but is generally accepted', according to Kate Colquhoun in *Taste: The Story of Britain through its Cooking*. His biographer, N. A. M. Rodger, suggests the first sandwich was most likely consumed at his desk. Whatever its origin, the sandwich or 'sarnie' is now ranked as the favourite outdoor food of the British.

WHAT'S IN A PUB NAME?

THE HOGSHEAD:
Any large barrel (from Dutch *ockshood*, 'measure').

THE BEAR AND RAGGED STAFF:
Badge of the earls of Warwick, with reference to bear-baiting.

THE RED LION:
The name of over 600 pubs, it probably referred to a local coat
of arms, since the lion is second only to the cross in such crests.

THE WHITE HART:
The emblem of Richard II of England, who introduced legislation
compelling public houses to display a sign.

THREE CROWNS:
The arms of the Worshipful Company of Drapers, though it can
also refer to the three kings of the Bible.

Another beloved snack of walkers is 'trail mix', which you can make up using any combination of nuts and dried fruits. Try dried apricots and cranberries, apple and banana chips, hazelnuts and sunflower seeds.

On the other hand, you wouldn't want to fill up too much – do leave room for a well-earned cream tea.

Two bags of crisps are walking down an isolated country road in the driving rain. A car pulls up and the driver winds down his window and asks: 'Do you want a lift?'

The first bag of crisps replies: 'No thanks, it's OK – we're walkers!'

The more sadistic purveyors of torture equipment would be hard pressed to devise a nastier punishment than arriving at a little village after twenty miles of hard footslogging, only to find that the old inn advertised as offering a fine range of real ales and bar meals has now shut.

DAVID BATHURST, *THE BIG WALKS OF GREAT BRITAIN*

As Darkness Falls

Hand in hand with the river wound the path, until twilight began to drive her dusky flocks across the west, and a light wind knitted the aspen branches against a silver sky with a crescent moon...

Edward Thomas, *Oxford*

The End of the Day

Tony Kevin, in *Walking the Camino*, advises on the importance of deciding before you set out each day where you plan to finish your day's walk. 'Your body and mind need this information to pace themselves throughout the day.' Alfred Wainwright was also a proponent of this habit. 'One should always have a definitive objective, in a walk as in life.'

The sweet-smelling white flowers of the campion or *Lychnis vespertina* open in the evening to attract moths. It is also known as 'grandmother's nightcap'.

... at night, in the absence of electric light, we see the world in... a beautiful, silver nitrate monochrome.

WILL SELF, WRITING IN *THE INDEPENDENT ON SUNDAY*

Bats and Badgers

Badgers, being nocturnal, are most often spotted at dusk in forest, but are shy and won't venture out if they know you're there. They are colour-blind but have strong senses of smell and hearing, so to spot one, find a sett and stand downwind and silent. And don't forget: its claws make it a fearsome fighter if provoked.

Belonging to the same family as the weasel and the stoat, the badger is Britain's largest land carnivore, and fossils of its bones have been found dating back 250,000 years. The old English name for badger was 'brock', giving rise to place names such as Brockenhurst.

Bats are not blind; they can see better than humans in the dark, and are the only mammals that fly. There are 17 species in Britain, ranging in size from the common pipistrelle, which weighs only 5 grams, to the common noctule, with a wingspan of up to 45 cm. You are most likely to see a bat in fading light as it flashes past. Daubenton's bat is often found near water. The brown long-eared bat has fluffy brown fur on top and large ears. You will only see the greater and lesser horseshoe bats, with their noses shaped like horseshoes, in south Wales and south-west England.

'When there's a ring around the moon
    Rain or snow is coming soon'
Altostratus or cirrostratus clouds containing ice crystals cause the moon to look watery or blurred, or wear a halo. This means rain is on its way, so you'll need a waterproof shelter for the night.

Off the B&B Track

The Mountain Bothies Association is a charity whose volunteers maintain approximately one hundred basic shelters in remote parts of the UK, mostly Scottish Highlands, keeping them open for anyone to use. The name 'bothy' may derive from the Gaelic *bothan*, small hut, or the Welsh *bwthyn*, small cottage, or perhaps even the Norse *buð*, from which we have the English word 'booth'. In the Alps, similar shelters called *Biwakschachtel* are managed by the Alpine Clubs.

The bivvy bag is a waterproof sack that will serve as an emergency shelter for you and your sleeping bag. Get a nice breathable Gortex one and you can zip it over your head to stay really warm, though it may be disorientating when you wake in the night. The bivvy bag lets you camp down anywhere while staying dry and snug. Your backpack will need its own bivvy bag, though.

The tarp tent is a plastic or nylon sheet that acts like a basic tent (held in place with guy ropes) but weighs and costs little. As a shelter it's very basic, with little protection from the elements, though more sophisticated ones now have storm flaps and bug screens, and even floors.

If the evening be fine and warm, there is nothing better in life than to lounge before the inn door in the sunset, or lean over the parapet of the bridge, to watch the weeds and the quick fishes... Your muscles are so agreeably slack, you feel so clean and so strong and so idle, that whether you move or sit still, whatever you do is done with pride and a kingly sort of pleasure.

ROBERT LOUIS STEVENSON

Walking Down Your Street: City Walks

*No fear of forgetting the good-humoured faces
that meet us in our walks each day.*

Mary Russell Mitford, *Our Village*

WALKS IN LONDON

London is a perfect city to wander around, with its winding streets, low skyline, parks and blue heritage plates everywhere. Since Charles Dickens was himself an enthusiastic walker, why not follow in his footsteps?

Start at 48 Doughty Street, now a museum, where he lived from 1837–1839, and continue via Gray's Inn, where he earlier worked as a clerk. Take in Fleet Prison, where Mr Pickwick is imprisoned for debt, Saffron Hill, the site of Bill Sikes's local in *Oliver Twist*, the site of the Saracen's Head Tavern of *Nicholas Nickleby* at Snow Hill, and the Old Bailey, once Newgate Prison, where Fagin was hanged. Other places featured in Dickens novels are St Paul's, the George and Vulture Inn, and Borough Market, where many streets are named after Dickens' characters. His father was imprisoned for debt at Marshalsea here. The George Inn is the only surviving galleried coaching inn in London, as featured in *Little Dorritt*, and an apt place to quench your thirst at the end of the walk.

48 Doughty Street

Johnny Borrell, singer, said in *The Times* that when his band Razorlight was just starting out and supporting the Libertines, he and the other band members would walk around London for hours out of necessity. It wasn't always everyone's idea of fun, but if anyone complained, the co-lead singer at the time, Carl Barât, would answer 'that if Charles Dickens walked ten miles a day, so could we'.

STROLL:

To walk about in a leisurely manner; to wander from place to place; a leisurely walk. Seventeenth century, probably from dialect German strollen, of obscure origin; compare German *Strolch* (tramp).

Often found in churchyards, the yew tree was an emblem of the soul's immortality to the Druids. On the other hand, it is connected with death, its berries yielding lethal poison and its foliage deadly to horses and cattle. Fenmen believed that witches sheltered under yew trees, and yew wood is popular for making magic wands. In Spain, yew is hung from balconies to protect from fire, while in the north of England a yew twig was thought to help you find something you had lost.

Yews have reddish brown bark which peels away easily, with branches growing up from the base and joining with the trunk, and dark green foliage.

In urban areas in Britain, people walk to accomplish their daily routine; walking in Inner London accounts for over 40 per cent of all trips. The Pedestrians' Association believes that walking is essential to halting the decline of urban areas and instead making them flourish. England's second city, Birmingham, was dominated for years by roads and flyovers, forcing pedestrians into unpleasant, threatening subways. Since the 1980s, the city centre has gradually become almost traffic-tree, improved with tree-lined boulevards. 'The streets throng with people even in winter, confounding those who believe that a thriving street life requires a Mediterranean climate or culture.' By creating a centre people want to enjoy, the regeneration strategy is bringing jobs, retailing and housing back to the city centre, showing walking can be important to creating a community, and 'a key indicator of its social, economic and cultural health.'

OPENDEMOCRACY.NET

GREAT CITY WALKS

Stratford-upon-Avon – explore Shakespeare's heritage on the walking routes

York – follow the Ebor Way from York Minster down the Ouse to Bishopthorpe Palace

Birmingham – walking guides help you explore the Victorian canals and Jewellery Quarter

Cambridge – follow the River Cam to the tearoom and pubs of Grantchester

Manchester – walk the towpath of the Rochdale Canal from the west end of Deansgate, past the building of the legendary Hacienda club, to the ultra-modern New Islington

Liverpool – take a guided walk around the sites of music legends from the Beatles to the Coral

Bath – learn what the city was like when Jane Austen wrote by visiting Bath Abbey, Pulteney Bridge, Queen Square, Royal Victoria Park, the Circus and Assembly Rooms

The only way I can keep hold of the old Manchester that I loved is by walking around it – I can see the places that survived, and the old textile buildings which are now hotels, restaurants and shops.

PETER HOOK IN *THE TIMES*

The American Podiatric Medical Association (APMA), *Prevention* magazine and Sperling's Great Places ranked the 100 most populous cities in the US against 19 criteria for walkability, including population density per square mile, public transport, crime rates and square miles of parks. 2009's Top Ten were:

San Francisco, CA
Boston, MA
New York, NY
Philadelphia, PA
Chicago, IL
Washington, DC
Seattle, WA
Honolulu, HI
Portland, OR
Pittsburgh, PA

Walking on Sunshine: Summer

And shadie seates, and sundry flowring bankes,
To sit and rest the walkers wearie shankes.

EDMUND SPENSER, *THE FAERIE QUEENE*

SUMMER FLOWERS:

Campions	Buttercups
Cow parsley	Clover
Stitchwort	Foxgloves
Dog daisies	Celandine

FLOWER POWER

Greater celandine, a member of the poppy family, is a yellow flower found by roadsides. Its botanical name *Chelidonium* means 'swallow', and you can see both flower and bird during the summer.

Several varieties of daisy grow wild in Britain: the Common daisy, the much larger Oxeye daisy (heads up to 6 cm across, stems up to 1 m), the Corn chamomile (heads up to 3 cm across and a pleasant smell), Hemp agrimony (up to 1.5 m high, with large clusters of pinky-white flowers) which grows near water, and coltsfoot, which resembles a Common daisy crossed with a dandelion.

Old Man's Beard, otherwise known as Traveller's Joy, is a bush of *Clematis vitalba* and its fruits are white and feathery. It blooms from July to August.

*When I go out into the countryside
and see the sun and the green
and everything flowering,
I say to myself, 'yes indeed,
all that belongs to me!'*

HENRI ROUSSEAU

HEDGEHOG

The hedgehog, with his thousands of spines made from hardened hairs, hibernates from October to April, so look for him in the summer. A nocturnal creature, he eats slugs, worms and beetles and lives around leaves and brushwood. Badgers eat hedgehogs, so you won't find hedgehogs where you find badgers.

Thou grimmest far o gruesome tykes
Grubbin thy food by thorny dykes
Gude faith, thou disna want for pikes
Baith sharp an rauckle;
Thou looks (Lord save's) arrayed in spikes,
A creepin heckle.

SAMUEL THOMPSON, FROM 'TO A HEDGEHOG'

Walking in warm weather is thirsty work. Keep your water supply chilled by freezing bottles of water overnight before you head out. By the time you're ready for your first water break, the ice will have melted but the water will still be refreshingly cold.

One thing is certain about going outdoors.
When you come back in, you'll be scratching.

P. J. O'ROURKE

CAMPING

If walking in summer, camping is not only a good budget option for staying out longer – it's a way to make the most of the outdoors.

Most long-distance footpaths and all national parks have campsites, and in the summer a farmer or pub might open up their land for campers.

In Australasia and North America wilderness camping is widely accepted; however, except in remote parts of Scotland, where the code of the Mountaineering Council applies, you need the landowner's permission in Britain.

If you do camp wild, be careful about cleanliness, leaving the site as you found it. Your toilet should be at least 100 metres away from water, and you should avoid camping too close to a river.

DOCK LEAVES

Dock leaves relieve the sting of a nettle, which you get by brushing against its hairs (grasp the nettle to avoid a sting) on footpaths and in hedgerows in summer. Dock always grows nearby and its leaves have a cooling effect:

In dock, out nettle,
Don't let the blood settle!

The hills were cloudy with woods in the heat... For the most part we saw only the great hawthorn hedge, which gave us the sense of a companion always abreast of us, yet always cool and fresh as if just setting out. It was cooler when a red-hot bicyclist passed by. A sombre river, noiselessly sauntering seaward, far away dropped with a murmur, among leaves, into a pool.... All things were lightly powdered with gold, by a lustre that seemed to have been sifted through gauze...

EDWARD THOMAS, *OXFORD*

FAMOUS WALKER: BRUCE CHATWIN

My God is the God of Walkers. If you walk hard enough, you probably don't need any other god.

Wanderer Bruce Charles Chatwin was born to a middle-class family in 1940 in Sheffield. Educated at Marlborough College, he had a strong interest in the classics and acting, and a hobby of restoring old furniture which led to his being made a director of Sotheby's in his twenties. He left there after eight years, disillusioned with the art business, and went to Edinburgh University to study archaeology, but left after two years without taking his degree and went to Mauritania.

There, he took many photographs of the desert and notes about the nomadic people, inspiring him to journeys in Iran, Afghanistan and Sudan. His fascination with nomads endured and he eventually adopted a travelling way of life, while writing about the importance of walking and the dangers of settlement.

Leaving a stint as a journalist on The Sunday Times magazine, it is said that he merely sent a telegram: 'Gone to Patagonia for six months'.

Patagonia always fascinated him because it was the farthest place a man could walk to. *In Patagonia* was Chatwin's first book of many on wide-ranging subjects, and it brought him literary acclaim. In 1987, he published *The Songlines*, an exploration of Aboriginal creation myths, which incorporated some of his early speculations about nomads. In an essay dedicated to the German film director Werner Herzog, Chatwin wrote that he was the only person with whom he could talk about 'what I would call the sacramental aspect of walking'; they shared the belief that walking is 'not simply therapeutic for oneself but is a poetic activity that can cure the world of its ills'.

He was also a friend of Patrick Leigh Fermor, and according to biographer Nicholas Shakespeare, on one of their walks Leigh Fermor told him the Latin expression solvitur ambulando – it is solved by walking – 'and immediately Bruce whipped out his notebook.'

He died in Nice, France, and his ashes were taken to Greece.

EXOTIC WALKS

*There is nothing like walking to
get the feel of a country.*

PAUL SCOTT MOWRER

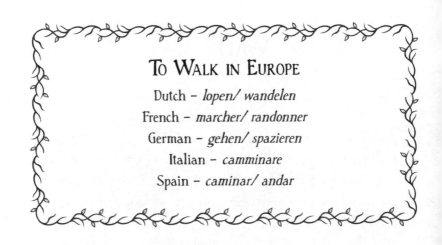

TO WALK IN EUROPE

Dutch – *lopen/ wandelen*

French – *marcher/ randonner*

German – *gehen/ spazieren*

Italian – *camminare*

Spain – *caminar/ andar*

The knowledge of the world is only to be acquired in the world, and not in a closet.

LORD CHESTERFIELD, IN A LETTER TO HIS SON

Eric Newby (1919–2006) entertained armchair travellers with his now classic book *A Short Walk in the Hindu Kush*, first published in 1958, which described a comically amateur expedition by himself and his friend Hugh Carless to scale a mountain of 20,000 feet (6,100 metres) in Afghanistan. From the outset, he declared how unprepared he was. He had of course done hill walking, and some mild 'scrambling in the Dolomites with my wife, but nowhere had we failed to encounter ladies twice our age armed with umbrellas.'

*Summiting Nevado Mismi was an obvious high
point. Looking out across the Amazon basin
knowing I'd be walking for the next two
years was overwhelmingly exciting.*

ED STAFFORD ON WALKING THE LENGTH OF THE AMAZON RIVER

In The Hills of Adonis: A Quest in Lebanon,
*Colin Thubron describes the intoxication of
walking through the orchards of Sidon during
the orange and lemon harvest and comments:
'Lebanon is half the size of Wales and is best
seen as centuries of people knew it,
on foot or on a donkey...'*

COLIN THUBRON, *THE HILLS OF ADONIS: A QUEST IN LEBANON*

UNIQUE WALKING PATHS OF THE WORLD

There are designated walking trails all over the world. Here's a sample:

Plitvice Lakes National Park, Croatia – a limestone canyon created over 10,000 years, with caves and forest and waterfalls.

Great Wall of China – stretching thousands of miles, this stone route offers hiking of all types including day trips from Beijing or more isolated sections meandering over hills.

Madeira, Portugal – follow cliff-edge aqueducts clinging to the edge of sheer chasms, or more gentle *levadas* through a land of heather, lily of the valley and wild orchids.

Negev, Israel – follow the *wadis* or dry streambeds through Biblical deserts where you might see ibex among the acacias.

South Luangwa National Park, Zambia – the birthplace of the walking safari, where you can stay in bush camps and see elephant, buffalo and antelope.

Oman – you can trek all year round above 1,900 metres in the mountainous landscape, including the Rim Walk of the Grand Canyon of Jabal Shams.

The Great Wall of China

I retrieved my backpack, and the monk pointed me in the right direction... The summer rain and sunshine kept the forested hills sparkling deep green. Brilliant leafy valleys stretched out before me, and I had only the dragonflies for company.

JENNIFER BARCLAY, *MEETING MR KIM*

The Philosopher's Walk

*All truly great thoughts
are conceived by walking.*

Friedrich Nietzsche

The Philosopher's Walk in Kyoto, Japan, was the route which Nishida Kitaro, one of the country's most famous philosophers, walked daily to the university. The stone path through the northern Higashiyama district begins near the Silver Pavilion and follows a canal lined by cherry trees, which explode with colour in April.

The Philosopher's Walk, Kyoto, Japan

Another Philosopher's Walk may be found in the street where Immanuel Kant lived. Born in 1724 in Prussia, he became a professor of philosophy acclaimed throughout Europe without ever leaving his home town. It is said that people would set their watches by when he left home for a walk every afternoon at 3.30 p.m.

Coleridge has told me that he himself liked to compose in walking over uneven ground, or breaking through the straggling branches of a copse-wood; whereas Wordsworth always wrote (if he could) walking up and down a straight gravel-walk.

WILLIAM HAZLITT

Walking is the natural recreation for a man who desires not absolutely to suppress his intellect but to turn it out to play for a season.

LESLIE STEPHEN

Heidelberg in Germany is home to one of Europe's oldest universities, dating to 1386. On the northern side of the river Neckar is a Philosopher's Walk, *Philosophenweg*, dedicated to the teachers and philosophers who walked and talked along the route over the centuries.

Aristotle's school of philosophy in Athens was named the Peripatetic School because he found that pacing up and down helped him to debate.

Walking is also an ambulation of mind.

GRETEL EHRLICH

You don't need to go to film school. You can learn the technical things in less than a week. All the rest you can learn by travelling on foot.

WERNER HERZOG, FILM DIRECTOR,
WHO ONCE WALKED FROM BERLIN TO PARIS

Buddhists believe that meditation does not have to be done sitting down, and well documented alternative approach for those who get restless is walking. In *The Benefits of Walking Meditation*, Sayadaw U. Silananda says that although there is no definite record that the Buddha gave specific instructions for walking meditation it is believed that he must have given such instructions at some time, which were then learned by his disciples and passed on down the generations. You must slow down and pay close attention to all of the movements involved, thinking about such things as the lightness of the foot and the breaths in and out. As with all Buddhist meditation, the idea is to bring one fully into awareness of the present moment.

You must walk like a camel, which is said to be the only beast which ruminates when it walks.

HENRY DAVID THOREAU, *A WRITER'S JOURNAL*

I can only meditate when I am walking. When I stop, I cease to think; my mind works only with my legs.

JEAN-JACQUES ROUSSEAU

BEST FOOT FORWARD

New boots are agony at first, so for goodness'
sake don't set off on a major expedition
in a pair of boots you only wore
to try on round the shop.

DAVID BATHURST, *THE BIG WALKS OF GREAT BRITAIN*

To soothe tired feet, try a spice bath in your socks. Mix a pinch of warming cayenne pepper with a smaller pinch of muscle-relaxing ginger powder, sprinkle in some old socks and wear normally. Take care to keep the mix away from eyes and cuts, and wash hands thoroughly after touching. Baking soda is also great for soaking tired feet at the end of a walking day – and it doubles up as a boot deodoriser.

I went into what I believe libel lawyers call 'a well-known Knightsbridge store' and bought six pairs of stout socks in pure wool. One pair wore into holes during the first day's walking, and none of the other five pairs survived as long as a week.

BERNARD LEVIN, *FROM THE CAMARGUE TO THE ALPS*

WALKER'S WISDOM

From *Take a Spare Truss: Essential Tips for Intrepid Nineteenth-Century Travellers* edited by Simon Brett:

It not unfrequently happens that the feet of those not thoroughly accustomed to hard tramping will become blistered. When the eggs of either poultry or wild birds are to be obtained, it is a good plan to break one or two, according to their size, into each shoe before starting in the morning.

LORD & BAINES

Rub the Feet at going to Bed with Spirits mixed with Tallow dropped from a lighted Candle into the palm of the hand. On the following morning no blister will exist. The Spirits seem to possess the healing power, the Tallow serving only to keep the skin soft and pliant. The Soles of the Feet, the Ancles, and Insteps, should be rubbed well; and even when no blisters exist, the application may be useful as a preventive: and while on this head, I would recommend foot travellers never to wear right and left Shoes – it is bad economy, and indeed serves to cramp the feet.

JOHN DUNDAS COCHRANE, *NARRATIVE OF A PEDESTRIAN JOURNEY THROUGH RUSSIA AND SIBERIAN TARTARY*

A warm footbath with bran will be found soothing after a long day's march. Soaping the inside of the stocking is another well-known safeguard against abrasion of the skin.

Baedecker, *The Eastern Alps*

SOCK IT TO ME

In socks, acrylic mixed with cotton or wool is ideal when it comes to socks to absorb moisture and take it away from the skin while providing cushioning, with flat seams around the toes. Foot powders can help to keep the feet dry.

Tony Kevin, in *Walking the Camino*, advises that to avoid blisters while walking all day in the heat, wear two pairs of walking socks; halfway through the day, remove your walking boots and socks, let your feet dry and rest propped high on a bench or your pack, which will cool them 'and ease the swelling'. Other tips include keeping your toenails trim (but not too short), and ensuring your laces and the tongue of your boots are well arranged.

If you feel painful friction (rather than a good wearing to toughen your feet), try to cushion as soon as possible using a plaster or 'moleskin' or a spray-on remedy. Thin liner socks help with getting new boots to fit properly.

In boots, look for good support underfoot and around the ankles, a sole with widely spaced treads and a stepped heel, and a waterproof upper.

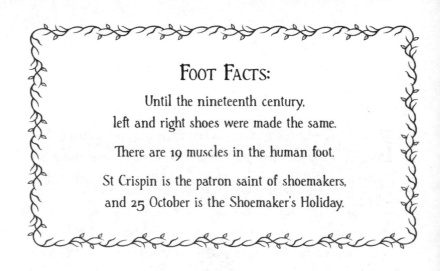

FOOT FACTS:

Until the nineteenth century,
left and right shoes were made the same.

There are 19 muscles in the human foot.

St Crispin is the patron saint of shoemakers,
and 25 October is the Shoemaker's Holiday.

'Merde,' *he gasped, giving me hope that he*
would order me off the road. Instead, he told
me that under no circumstances must I quit
walking, even for an hour. 'Eef you stop,' *he*
said gravely, 'your feet has won.'

CHARLES WILKINS, *WALK TO NEW YORK*

An unfortunate hiker experiencing leg pains hobbles into a doctor's office.

'Doctor, my right leg is killing me. Can you take a look at it?'

The doctor puts his stethoscope to the man's right shin bone, and hears a tiny voice say 'Doc, can you lend me a pound?'

Shaking his head, he then puts his stethoscope to the man's knee joint, and hears another voice say 'Doctor, can you spare any change?'

Looking very serious, he moves his stethoscope higher to the hiker's thigh. Listening carefully, he hears 'Doctor, could you spare the price of a cup of coffee?'

The doctor puts down the stethoscope and sighs.

'What is it?' asks the hiker.

'I'm sorry to say it, but your leg's broke in three places.'

GOING THE DISTANCE

*If you are for a merry jaunt, I will try,
for once, who can foot it farthest.*

JOHN DRYDEN

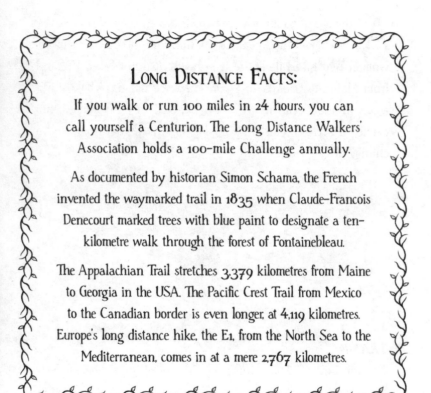

LONG DISTANCE FACTS:

If you walk or run 100 miles in 24 hours, you can call yourself a Centurion. The Long Distance Walkers' Association holds a 100-mile Challenge annually.

As documented by historian Simon Schama, the French invented the waymarked trail in 1835 when Claude-Francois Denecourt marked trees with blue paint to designate a ten-kilometre walk through the forest of Fontainebleau.

The Appalachian Trail stretches 3,379 kilometres from Maine to Georgia in the USA. The Pacific Crest Trail from Mexico to the Canadian border is even longer, at 4,119 kilometres. Europe's long distance hike, the E1, from the North Sea to the Mediterranean, comes in at a mere 2,767 kilometres.

At the age of 71, Emma Gatewood saw a *National Geographic* article about the Appalachian Trail and, discovering that no woman had hiked its entire length, successfully hiked the trail from Maine to Georgia in 1958. Then she did the whole thing again in 1960. And in 1963. She walked in tennis shoes and carried a blanket, plastic sheet, cup, first aid kit, raincoat and a change of clothes.

TRAMP:
To walk long and far; hike. To walk heavily or firmly across or through; march or trudge. To wander about as a vagabond or tramp. To make a journey or traverse a place on foot…

The 'End to End' is a common way of referring to the walk from Land's End in England to John O'Groats in Scotland, the two points furthest apart on the British mainland (approximately 868 miles). Bill Butlin, the holiday camp entrepreneur, organised the first End to End charity walk.

If you pick 'em up,
O Lord, I'll put 'em down.

PRAYER OF THE TIRED WALKER

In July 1994 I stood on Tower Bridge in an euphoric moment of achievement. I had joined a select band of people who have walked the entire length of Britain's coast... Two years later I became pregnant, was left by the father, gave birth to my son and, four months later, was diagnosed with cancer. These events were to take me on an emotional journey which involved more pain, tears and fatigue than walking Britain's coast ever could. In an effort to come to terms with all this, I did what felt best and went for a walk.

SPUD TALBOT-PONSONBY,
SMALL STEPS WITH PAWS AND HOOVES: A HIGHLAND JOURNEY

PILGRIMAGE

Santiago de Compostela in Galicia, north-west Spain, was Europe's most famous centre of pilgrimage in the Middle Ages, and in recent years the pilgrims' paths to Santiago crossing Spain and Portugal have enjoyed a revival.

Of many alternative routes, most popular is *Camino Frances*, the French Way, from Vezelay, Le Puy or Arles in France (Notre Dame des Tables in Montpellier was named for the money-changers who catered for pilgrims passing through), across the Pyrenees and across northern Spain.

Via de la Plata starts in Seville in the south, from where it is 1000 kilometres to Santiago. Walkers stay at hostels or *albergues por los peregrinos* where you can get a stamp in your book at the end of each day to qualify for a certificate at the end; stamps can also be given at churches and monasteries. The pilgrimage is taken seriously. Tony Kevin writes in *Walking the Camino*, the ecclesiastical authorities might take less kindly to 'a pilgrim's *credencial* that looks like nothing more than evidence of a sustained pub-crawl across Spain'.

The Ridgeway path 'is in some sort humanly companionable: it really seems to lead you by the hand'.

KENNETH GRAHAME

FAMOUS WALKER: PATRICK LEIGH FERMOR

who walked from Holland to Constantinople

Sir Patrick 'Paddy' Michael Leigh Fermor, sometimes called 'Britain's greatest living travel writer', was born in 1915. His father was a distinguished geologist, and not long after Patrick was born, his mother left to join his father in India, leaving him with another family. At school he resisted academic structure, and was sent to a school for difficult children. Expelled from the King's School, Canterbury, when caught holding hands with a local greengrocer's daughter, he educated himself from there on, reading Greek, Latin, Shakespeare and History with hopes of entering Sandhurst.

However, at the age of 18 he decided instead to walk the length of Europe, 'like a tramp, a pilgrim, or a wandering scholar', from the Hook of Holland to Constantinople. He set off on 8 December

1933 with just a few clothes, the *Oxford Book of English Verse* and volume of Horace's *Odes*. He slept in hayricks and shepherds' huts, but also in the castles and country houses of aristocracy. He commented that the Hungarians were amused and impressed by his journey: 'Nobody else was travelling like this in those days.'

After his return, he became a soldier and played a prominent role behind the lines in the Battle of Crete during World War Two; at the age of 25, as an SOE agent, he kidnapped the German commander of Crete.

Fermor has been working on the trilogy based on his journey on and off for nearly 70 years. It was only in 2007 that he finally agreed to use a typewriter, previously preferring to write everything in longhand. Often called his masterpiece, *A Time of Gifts* was only published in 1977, and *Between the Woods and the Water* nine years later; both show his scholarly learning, giving a wealth of historical, geographical, linguistic and anthropological information. The narrative of the final section of the journey to Constantinople has been eagerly awaited for decades. He now lives in Greece.

WALKING IN THE RAIN:
AUTUMN

Rain is one thing the British
do better than anybody else.

MARILYN FRENCH

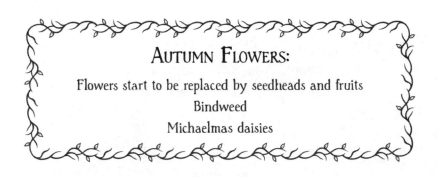

AUTUMN FLOWERS:

Flowers start to be replaced by seedheads and fruits

Bindweed

Michaelmas daisies

Bindweed is found from late summer in hedges and bushes; it is also known as hedge-strangler, referring to its long trailing stems, or bellbine, referring to the large bell-like white flowers.

Till St Swithin's Day be past,
The apples be not fit to taste.

FOLK SAYING

St Swithin's Day is 15 July, and when his bones were moved from the old cathedral at Winchester in AD 970, he wept so much that rain followed for forty days. The rain is said to 'christen' or help the apples.

Trees rest during winter, when there is not enough light or water for photosynthesis (turning water and carbon dioxide into oxygen and glucose for energy for growing); they shut down the food-making process and live off the food stored during the summer. With no need for the green chlorophyll, the chemical that makes photosynthesis happen, it disappears from the leaves, revealing the orange (xanthophyll) and yellow (carotene) colours that were there all along but covered up by chlorophyll. In some trees, like maples, glucose trapped in the leaves after the photosynthesis stops is turned red by the sunlight and cool nights of autumn. Other leaves like oak turn brown because of waste left over. When leaves have no water supply and no food made in them, they start to die, and as the orange and yellow fade also, the leaf becomes brown, dry and crunchy. Just perfect underfoot!

Westonbirt Arboretum in Gloucestershire has more than 17,000 exotic trees from all over the world, including Japanese maples, whose leaves turn bright red and yellow in the autumn.

FORAGING FOR CHESTNUTS

Gather plump, dark brown sweet chestnuts in the woods in autumn. The shells look a little like horse chestnut or conker shells – green and spiky – but don't eat conkers (as all parts of the horse chestnut are poisonous, causing vomiting). Those out of their shells are most likely to be ready for eating, so no need to prick your fingers.

To roast them, cut a cross with a knife to stop them exploding, sprinkle with water and put them in the oven in a baking tray at 200 Celsius for about 20 minutes. Take them out, give the tray a shake, sprinkle with more water and put back in for another 10 minutes or until the shells start to come apart. Peel while still hot using a tea towel and squeezing the shell. An alternative cooking method is in a frying pan with holes drilled in, shaking constantly, for that 'cooked over an open fire' taste.

Sweet chestnut

Horse chestnut

Season of mists and mellow fruitfulness.

JOHN KEATS

Another excellent place to walk in the autumn is Ashdown Forest in East Sussex – where A. A. Milne was inspired to write *Winnie-the-Pooh*. Artefacts found there suggest the area has been occupied as far back as the Middle Palaeolithic period, around 50,000 years ago, and in Norman times it was a deer hunting forest, while artists and writers inspired by the woods include Ivor Hitchens, Edmund J. Niemann and John Piper. It is now the largest free public access space in the South East, in the heart of the High Weald, and protected for its wildlife. Nearly two thirds of its 6,500 acres are rare heathland, and bird life to be spotted there includes the hen harrier and the great grey shrike.

BLACKBERRIES

There is something very satisfying about searching through the tangle of thorns for sweet, juicy blackberries. They contain lots of antioxidants and high levels of folic acid. Here's a recipe to make if you take the blackberries home with you.

Blackberry Sorbet
450 g blackberries
150 ml water
150 g sugar
Juice of two and a half lemons
A splash (2 tablespoons) of something like crème de mûre (or damson gin)

Wash and dry the berries, then put them in a pan with the sugar and water and bring to the boil, simmering for 2–3 minutes until the fruit has started to release its juice. Cool, then liquidise and strain or just push through a sieve to remove the seeds and debris. Add the alcohol and the lemon juice, cover and chill, then pour into a shallow plastic container and put in the freezer. Take it out every hour and break up the ice crystals formed around the edge with a fork until it's the consistency of a Slush Puppy – about 4 stirrings – and then leave in the freezer to firm up. Take it out about 20 minutes before you want to eat.

If it's too cold for sorbet, add blackberries to muesli or porridge in the morning, or keep the berries in the freezer and just add to yoghurt or juice to make smoothies. Delicious and healthy.

On Michaelmas, 29 September, by legend, the Devil spits on blackberries or puts his cloven hoof on them, making them inedible. There is a lot of tannin in brambles and perhaps when they start to wither, they are too bitter. In Brittany there are taboos against picking blackberries because of their association with fairies, and in Majorca they are associated with the Crown of Thorns. But in England and America, diseases could be cured by passing through the arch of a blackberry rooted at either end.

FOOTING IT
THROUGH FARMS

Walking connects you to the land.

KELLY WINTERS

Formed in 1935, the Ramblers' Association campaigns to protect rights of way in Britain and the natural beauty of the countryside. Members also help to waymark rights of way and install and repair stiles and bridges. The 'right to roam' allows access to hills and mountains, rivers and lakes, through valleys and across moors. We can be grateful to the Ramblers' Association for many of our long distance paths and national parks.

As Bill Bryson wrote in *Walk* magazine, 'If you announced that you intended to amble across Iowa cornfields for pleasure, people would think you were out of your mind.' And yet in Britain we can walk through farmland because of footpaths, stiles, maps and a tradition of public access...

*The farmer allows walkers
across the field for free,
but the bull charges.*

SIGN ON AN IRISH GATE

*I like to see something in the distance – a
green hill, a fine tree, a farmhouse, a church, a
man plying a scythe – and approach slowly
on foot rather than rush towards it on wheels.*

BERNARD LEVIN, *FROM THE CAMARGUE TO THE ALPS*

Black and white cows are Holstein Friesians; they derive from Germany and Holland, but now account for most of the cows seen in British fields. If you see something very similar but brown and white, it's a Guernsey, or an Ayrshire if the markings are less evenly distributed. The Jersey is fawn with a dark patch down the front of its head.

Then there are the beef herds, the bulls; most common in Britain being the black Aberdeen Angus, followed by the Swiss Simmental, brown with occasional white patches. The Charolais from central France are white all over, and the Limousin, also French, are rusty-brown with white faces.

When cows all sit down together in a sheltered valley, it can mean that rain is on the way, especially if birds are also flying low in search of insects. Insects will settle when rain is on its way. Cows sense the rain due to electricity in the air.

COMMON BREEDS OF SHEEP:

Swaledale – white mountain sheep with black faces but white noses, ears and eye patches, and curly horns.

Cheviot – white hill sheep with no horns, ruff of wool around neck.

Romney – white with no horns, woolly on top of head, mainly SE England.

Suffolk – white, no horns, black head and legs.

Mule – white, brown and white mottled face, no horns.

Hark! how sweet the horned ewes bleat
On the solitary steeps

ALFRED LORD TENNYSON, 'THE LOTOS-EATERS'

A flock of mountain sheep watched us go,
making noises that sounded
suspiciously like laughter.

ERIC NEWBY, *A SHORT WALK IN THE HINDU KUSH*

And now here are the results of the Sheepdog Trials. All the sheepdogs were found not guilty.

Keith Waterhouse

COPPICING

Our ancient ancestors discovered that if you cut a tree down to its stump, small twigs would sprout, producing wood that is good for all manners of uses. The art almost died out with the advent of industry, but now it has been revived and you may easily see coppiced trees in the countryside. Coppiced hardwood trees such as hazel, ash, oak, willow, maple and sweet chestnut are good for producing gates, fences, charcoal, baskets, furniture – and walking sticks! Coppicing also stimulates the growth of spring flowers like violets, bluebells and primroses, and encourages dormice.

There's something about a farm that gets you...
particularly if the wind's in the wrong direction.

JANET ROGERS

EQUIPMENT

*There's no such thing as the wrong weather,
just the wrong clothes.*

JULIA BRADBURY,
TV PRESENTER OF *COUNTRYFILE* AND *WAINWRIGHT WALKS*

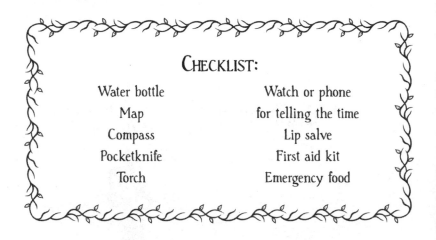

CHECKLIST:

Water bottle

Map

Compass

Pocketknife

Torch

Watch or phone

for telling the time

Lip salve

First aid kit

Emergency food

With a well-packed and well-adjusted rucksack, you can forget you are carrying anything – until the end of the day.

TONY KEVIN, *WALKING THE CAMINO*, ON ADJUSTING A BACKPACK

To walk with a heavy pack, cinch up the wait belt until it's snug around your hips to take the weight off your shoulders. Clip the chest strap to prevent it from bouncing around. To keep your upper back and neck comfortable when carrying backpacks, shrug your shoulders up towards your ears then roll them down again – and repeat twenty times. This will also help you breathe deeply.

First into my backpack went my Swiss army knife, the official, full-sized, schoolboy's dream – two penknives, three screwdrivers, a bottle-opener, a tin-opener, a corkscrew, a saw, scissors, a file, a fish-scaler, a ruler, a wire-stripper, a magnifying-glass, tweezers, a toothpick and a thing for taking stones out of elephants' hooves; I was equipped for any ordinary emergency, and a good few unlikely ones as well.

BERNARD LEVIN, *FROM THE CAMARGUE TO THE ALPS*

STICK SENSE

Walking with poles or a cane or stick can reduce the striking force of feet hitting the ground considerably. Ideally it should be comfortable enough to feel like an extension of the walker's arm, and is a great help going up or down hills, especially where ground is slippery or rough. They also take some of the weight off the knees on descents. When crossing a slope, hold the stick in the upper hand, not the lower.

Michael P. Garofalo, in his 'Eighty Eight Ways of Walking', also recommends it for doing exercises along the way 'to improve your strength and flexibility in your shoulders and arms' – this should lead to a secondary benefit of scaring most other walkers away, leaving you with the path to yourself. Oh, and finally Garofalo adds that you can use it to 'defend yourself against animals or evil doers'.

Walking sticks are often made of the wood of the ash, and traditionally this is not only for its strength but for its magical qualities. It was thought to be best for killing snakes swiftly. Emigrants from Ireland to the United States in the nineteenth century carried twigs from a descendant of the sacred ash tree of Creevna to protect themselves from drowning. In the nineteenth century, an ash planted next to a sycamore warned coachmen of a crossroads ahead.

You won't want to nancy about in shorts once the first leech has had a go at you.

REDMOND O'HANLON RECOMMENDS JUNGLE BOOTS AND
THICK TROUSERS FOR WALKING, *INTO THE HEART OF BORNEO*

BASICS OF USING A COMPASS

The red part of the compass needle is always pointing towards the earth's magnetic North pole. The turnable part of the compass is called the housing, with a scale on the edge, and the letters N, S, W and E. If you want to go northwest, turn the compass housing so that northwest on the housing aligns with the direction of the travel arrow. Hold the compass flat in your hand so the needle can turn freely, then turn yourself around until the compass needle is aligned with the lines inside the housing, making absolutely sure that it is the red (North) part of the needle that points at North in the compass housing. Make sure also that nothing iron might be disturbing the arrow – even a staple in your map could affect it and send you off in the wrong direction. Once you are pointing in the right direction, aim at some point in the distance and put the compass away for a while.

These are basics: get yourself some proper detailed instructions before setting out into the unknown. A compass is a valuable piece of equipment, simple but powerful. Wherever you are on Earth, a compass in your hand will always point North and help you find the way. And unlike a GPS, it doesn't need batteries.

WATERSIDE WALKING

We could not walk as slowly as the river flowed; yet that seemed the true pace to move in life, and so reach the great grey sea.

EDWARD THOMAS, *OXFORD*

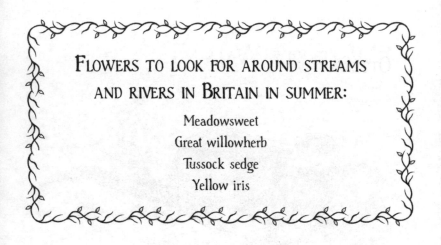

FLOWERS TO LOOK FOR AROUND STREAMS
AND RIVERS IN BRITAIN IN SUMMER:

Meadowsweet
Great willowherb
Tussock sedge
Yellow iris

Britain's network of canals and waterways were mostly built for carrying freight by horse-drawn barges before the days of engines, and the towpaths make ideal walking trails. Some have been turned into official National Waterway walks, such as the Kennet and Avon Canal between Bath and Reading. If you're not a fan of walking up or down hills, canal walks are ideal – and you can't get lost! Then there's the Thames Path, of course.

OTTERS

Solitary and water-loving, otters grow up to 1.2 m in length – much larger than polecats or minks, with dark brown coats, off-white throats and webbed feet. The male is a dog and the female a bitch. The collective name is a romp of otters.

VOLES AND OTHER RODENTS

Plumper than mice, with shorter tails and rounder heads. Bank voles are red-brown tree-climbers with a long tail; field voles shorter in the tail and greyer; water voles are larger, up to 22 cm, dark brown. Brown rats are much larger, although the black rat is small and very rare. Shrews, including the water shrew, are not rodents but more closely related to the hedgehog; their distinguishing features are tiny eyes and long pointed noses. Note to gardeners: they eat through their own body weight in insects, worms, slugs and snails every day.

*I hear the sound of Heywood's
Brook falling into Fair Haven Pond,
inexpressibly refreshing to my
senses. It seems to flow through
my very bones... Thus I am washed;
thus I drink and quench my thirst.
Where the streams fall into the lake,
if they are only a few inches more
elevated, all walkers may hear.*

HENRY DAVID THOREAU, *A WRITER'S JOURNAL*

The Marine and Coastal Access Act became law in England 12 November 2009, creating a continuous coastal access zone as well as protection for marine habitats. Nicholas Crane, presenter of the BBC's *Coast* series, wrote in the *Daily Telegraph* that 'every beach tells a story' and 'I can't be the only walker who'd love to follow an uninterrupted trail from Berwick-upon-Tweed to Newcastle, by way of Holy Island and Seahouses.'

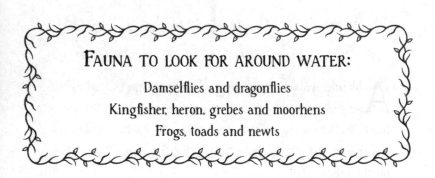

FAUNA TO LOOK FOR AROUND WATER:

Damselflies and dragonflies

Kingfisher, heron, grebes and moorhens

Frogs, toads and newts

When I was a kid in the seventies, we would sometimes walk into town on a Sunday and it would be quite ghostly... you still get that peaceful, otherworldly feel as you walk along its canals.

PETER HOOK IN *THE TIMES*

A blonde walker comes to a river and cannot see a bridge anywhere nearby. She spots another blonde on the opposite bank. 'Hello! I'm trying to figure out how to get to the other side!' she shouts. The other woman looks at her blankly. 'You're already on the other side!'

The herons themselves glided low and waded through the flagleaves with a jerky and purposeful gait, or, vigilantly on one leg like the storks, posed with cunning as plants.

PATRICK L. FERMOR, *BETWEEN THE WOODS AND THE WATER*

You'll Never Walk Alone?

One of the pleasantest things in the world is going on a journey; but I like to go by myself.

WILLIAM HAZLITT, *TABLE TALK*

If you go in company, or even in pairs, it is no longer a walking tour in anything but name; it is something else and more in the nature of a picnic. A walking tour should be gone upon alone, because freedom is of the essence; because you should be able to stop and go on, and follow this way or that, as the freak takes you; and because you must have your own pace, and neither trot alongside a champion walker, nor mince in time with a girl.

ROBERT LOUIS STEVENSON, *WALKING TOURS*

... the best thing of all is walking with the kids, at their pace. Going slow forces you to leave the world behind.

ALEX JAMES

Your companion must sympathize with the present mood... Farewell to those who will talk of nature unnaturally, whose presence is an interruption.

HENRY DAVID THOREAU, *A WRITER'S JOURNAL*

If a man does not keep pace with his companions, perhaps it is because he hears a different drummer.

HENRY DAVID THOREAU, *WALDEN: OR LIFE IN THE WOODS*

WALKING FESTIVALS

Tens of thousands of people walk along Britain's long-distance trails every year. If you enjoy walking in company, why not look up some of the walking festivals that happen all over these days, such as:

Madeira Islands Walking Festival – January

Crickhowell (UK) Walking Festival – February to March

International Two Days walk, Rororua (NZ) – March

Gilboa (Israel) Two Days – March to April

North Devon and Exmoor (UK) Walking Festival – April to May

Isle of Wight (UK) Walking Festival – May

International Two Days Marches of Flanders – May

Summer Walking Festival, Isle of Man (UK) – June

Castlebar (Ireland) Four Days Walks – July

Pendle (Lancashire, UK) Walking Festival – August

Mare e Monti Two Days March Arenzano (Italy) – September

Coniston (UK) Walking Festival – September

East Perthshire (UK) Walking Festival – October

US Freedom Walk Festival of Arlington (USA) – October

International Walk of Barcelona – October

Busan City (Korea) Walking Festival – November

Higashi–Matsuyama (Japan) Three Days March – November

Taipei Two Days Happiness March – November

Hereford (UK) Winter Walking Festival – December
(Check annually for details)

WALKIES!

Dogs are great walking companions. Here are some tips for walking with your trusty hound:

LEADING THE WAY:
If your dog is on a lead, it can't get away and chase animals; consider a pinch collar, harness or best of all a retractable lead to give the dog a little more slack.

LEFT OUT:
Call ahead to check to see if there are any restrictions on taking dogs where you plan to walk, including visitors' centres, shops or pubs. Stony paths are not always a favourite with dogs, especially on hot days.

LAPPING IT UP:
If there's no natural source of water, carry water for both of you. A plastic bag will work as a handy collapsible bowl.

CHILLING OUT:
Dogs can't sweat. In the summer, find a safe place to let your dog drink and cool down in some water, or a shady spot to rest for a while.

DON'T LOSE OUT:

Make sure your dog has a name tags, and in case it gets pulled off, consider backup ID such as an embedded microchip. Carry a photo in case your dog goes missing.

CHECK HIM OUT:

Check with your vet if your faithful friend has any medical or weight problems. Work up to the longer distances by doing shorter walks first.

The wonderful thing about having dogs is that it makes you go walking.

PEARL LOWE IN *THE TIMES*

Two ladies are out walking in the countryside. Edith suddenly bursts out:

'My, did you see that?'

'No,' answers Mabel, looking round. 'What was it?'

'An eagle just flew right above our heads!' said Edith, smugly. A few minutes later, she chirps once again, 'Golly! Did you see that Mabel?'

'What?' sighs Mabel, whose eyesight isn't what it used to be.

'It was a lesser-spotted pond-warbler, of course!' squeals Edith excitedly. 'What a shame you missed it.'

They continue in silence for ten minutes, before Edith says, 'Oh, Mabel, you must have seen that!'

'Yes, of course,' says Mabel, now more than a little irritated.

'Oh,' says Edith. 'Then why did you step in it?'

Avid walker and film-maker Werner Herzog is a proponent of solitude as a 'fundamental experience in life'. Patrick Leigh Fermor, in his long walk across Europe described in *Between the Woods and the Water*, wrote of how the walker can be kept company 'on lonely stretches' by poetry and songs that enter one's head. On the other hand, Mark Twain wrote that the 'true charm of pedestrianism does not lie in the walking, or in the scenery, but in the talking.'

If you take the path less travelled, maybe it's because you march to the beat of a different drum. On the other hand, maybe you're just completely lost.

PATRICK MURRAY

FAMOUS WALKER: HILAIRE BELLOC

The Poet Laureate of West Sussex, Hilaire Belloc was born on 27 July 1870 in St Cloud, outside Paris, of an English mother and French father. At the age of six, following the death of his father, his mother brought him and his sister Marie to England, at first to London. A few years later, she moved the family to Slindon in the West Sussex countryside, where began Belloc's love of the woods and downs, which was to stay with him for the rest of his life. In *The Hills and the Sea*, he writes of how, as a boy, he pushed through a beech forest, climbed over a glade called No Man's Land, 'and I was surprised and glad, because from the ridge of that glade I saw the sea.'

He served in the French army and then, after studying Modern History at Oxford, he and his American wife moved to Shipley in West Sussex, and lived in a rambling house with five acres of land and a windmill. His writing career began with books of verse for children. A friend of H. G. Wells and George Bernard Shaw, he was a public speaker, politician and journalist, and travelled in America, Cuba, Italy, Spain and the Holy Land.

Belloc is known in the walking fraternity for the story of his walk across Sussex, published in 1912 as *The Four Men*, as well as for *The Path to Rome*, 1902, an account of his solitary walking pilgrimage from central France across the Alps and down to Rome, which has remained continuously in print. It contains not only descriptions of the people and places he encountered, and drawings in pencil and in ink of the route, but also his personal reflections. Belloc cared passionately about the beauty of the landscape and country ways. In 1910, he published 'The South Country', verse referring to the 'great hills' that stand along the sea, 'And it's there walking in the high woods/ That I could wish to be.'

WALKIN' IN A WINTER WONDERLAND

When gorse is out of blossom,
Then kissing's out of fashion.

FOLK SAYING

*I prefer winter and fall, when you feel the bone
structure in the landscape – the loneliness of it
– the dead feeling of winter.*

ANDREW WYETH

*You can't beat a beautiful, life-affirming walk
through icy silver and green countryside.*

ALEX JAMES IN *THE TIMES*

WINTER FLOWERS:

Gorse

Snowdrops

First leaves of daffodils and bluebells

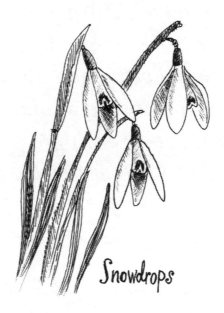

Snowdrops

*There is scarcely any earthly
object that gives me more – I don't
know if I should call it pleasure,
but something which exalts me,
something which enraptures me –
than to walk in the sheltered side
of a wood or high plantation, in
a cloudy winter day, and hear a
stormy wind howling among the
trees and raving o'er the plain.*

ROBERT BURNS

WALKING ON THIN ICE

Traditional snowshoes were made of a hardwood frame laced with rawhide, shaped like a tennis racquet to distribute the wearer's weight over a larger area to prevent sinking into deep snow. If you take a walk around Algonquin Park in Ontario, Canada, from a traditional log cabin, you may well end up wearing them to cross deeply frozen lakes. Modern snowshoes work on the same principle, but are made of lightweight metal and plastic which clips easily onto your boot; these often have spikes underneath for gripping ice when climbing, for example in the snowy mountains of France. They are still used by forest rangers, but also by hikers and runners in winter, though they can be hard on the calf muscles at first, with long use leading to what Canadian *voyageurs* would call *mal de raquette*.

The abrupt sides of vast mountains
were before me; the icy wall of the
glacier overhung me; a few shattered
pines were scattered around; and
the solemn silence of this glorious
presence-chamber of imperial
Nature was broken only by the
brawling waves, or the fall of some
vast fragment, the thunder sound
of the avalanche, or the cracking
reverberating along the mountains
of the accumulated ice...

MARY SHELLEY, *FRANKENSTEIN*

HOW TO BUILD A SNOW SHELTER

In firm snow, dig out a rough rectangle of snow just wider than yourself. With a pick-axe, draw a rectangle above it and dig out underneath the block, slide your hands underneath it and lift it out as neatly as possible. This is your first 'brick' to build the shelter: place it carefully on one side of the hole, and continue digging out further blocks and placing them around the edges, creating a trench with walls on either side and at the far end. Deeper snow will make deeper blocks. Now, the tricky part: for the roof, you'll need larger blocks – for this you'll need to dig a fresh 'quarry'. Finally, use loose snow to fill in cracks and holes in the walls. Insulate the floor with some clothing or a sack and crawl inside your new home!

A Walk on the Wild Side

Nature halts self-absorption, makes you less frantic about all that's going on in your own small mental or physical world.

Margaret Drabble

The fire was dying down by their campsite as Sherlock Holmes addressed Dr Watson. Holmes, lying on his blanket, asked: 'Watson, tell me what you see up there.'

'Ah, a wondrous array of brilliant stars,' replied Watson.

'And what, dear Watson, does that tell you?' asked Holmes.

Watson replied: 'It is testament to billions of other galaxies with similar densities of stars, possibly trillions of planets associated with them. With such numbers and a similar chemical distribution in all the cosmos, a man might infer the likelihood of intelligent life up there.

What's more, theologically, the great vastness of that wondrous space indicates the greatness of God, a reminder that we are mere mortals of minor significance.

If we consider the sky meteorologically, its blackness and the clear brilliance of the stars suggests decreased humidity and stable air, which could well lead to a clear day on the morrow.

Would you add more, Mr Holmes? What does the vision convey to you?'

'Well,' replied Holmes philosophically, 'looking up there, I'd conclude that somebody forgot to bring the tent.'

There's nothing more frustrating than building a first class campfire, then going to light it and discovering that your matches have gone soggy. You can avoid this annoying predicament by dipping the heads of non-safety matches in melted candle wax. Once set they can go back in the box ready for use. Your cleverly waterproofed matches will light when struck against any surface.

Recipe for Campfire Bread

Bannock originates from Scotland and was originally made with oats. The ingredients can be measured out at home and then carried mixed together in a plastic bag; nuts and berries found along the route can be added. You will need a large pan or cooking pot.

3 mugs flour
2 mugs milk powder
1 tsp baking powder
1 tsp sugar
1 mug water
Olive oil

When your campfire is hot, preferably hot embers with no flames, place the pan on it with a little oil to heat up. Add the water to the dry ingredients and mix well together in the bag, also adding any nuts or berries. Flatten the mixture to an inch thick and place on the hot oil, then fry for about 7 minutes on each side until golden. It will break easily by hand, with no need for a knife.

I felt my spirits rise when I had got off the road into the open fields, and the sky had a new appearance. I stepped along more buoyantly. There was a warm sunset over the wooded valleys, a yellowish tinge on the pines. Reddish dun-coloured clouds like dusky flames stood over it... Before I walked in the ruts of travel; now I adventured.

Henry David Thoreau, *A Writer's Journal*

LIFE IN THE WILDS

Weasels – gingery-brown.
Stoats – dull brown or white.
Polecats – yellowy-brown with white patches on face.
Pine martens – dark brown with big ears.
American minks – almost black.

All have long sleek bodies. Weasels and stoats are very adaptable
and can live mostly anywhere, whereas polecats prefer water and
woods, pine martens mainly forests, and minks mainly water.

*I saw nobody all day; there were numbers
of red squirrels, a few black ones,
and innumerable birds.*

PATRICK L. FERMOR *BETWEEN THE WOODS AND THE WATER*

NETTLE TEA

Nettles, with their hairy, saw-edged leaves, grow abundantly all over Britain all year and provide food for butterflies and birds. Pick the first top shoots of small, young nettles early in the year and make soup or tea for an excellent source of iron, calcium and folic acid. Wash to get rid of soil and insects, then put in a pot and add enough water to just about cover them. Boil until the water becomes slightly green and remove the nettles (the tea might go bitter if they are left in). The boiled nettles can be eaten with salt, like spinach. If possible, serve the tea with sugar and sliced lemons – the lemon changes its colour from dark green to bright pink!

To make nettle soup, cook with a knob of butter for ten minutes, mash the pulp, add garlic, cornflour, milk and seasoning.

In his introduction to A Short Walk in the Hindu Kush *by Eric Newby, Evelyn Waugh says the impetus which carried Newby was (and he apologises for the phrase) 'the call of the wild'. This he defines as the romantic and reasonless longing among most Englishmen 'to shun the celebrated spectacles of the tourist and... simply to set their feet where few civilised feet have trod'.*

EVELYN WAUGH, INTRODUCING *A SHORT WALK IN THE HINDU KUSH*

There were dozens of streams to drink from, many of them thick with watercress.

PATRICK L. FERMOR, *BETWEEN THE WOODS AND THE WATER*

FOR THE LOVE
OF A GOOD WALK

*The great affair is to move; to feel the needs
and hitches of our life more nearly; to come
down off this feather-bed of civilisation, and
find the globe granite underfoot and
strewn with cutting flints.*

ROBERT LOUIS STEVENSON

Within 10 miles of wherever you are sitting now there is almost certainly countryside to take your breath away.

BILL BRYSON IN *WALK* MAGAZINE

The rain and sun alternating are like two lovers in dialogue; the rain smiles from the hills when the sun shines, and the sun also while the rain is falling. When the rain is not over and the sun has interrupted, the nightingale sings, where the stitchwort is starry amidst long grass that bathes the sweeping branches of thorn and brier; and I am now stabbed, and now caressed, by its changing song...

EDWARD THOMAS, *OXFORD*

Now I yearn for one of those old, meandering, dry, uninhabited roads, which lead away from towns, which lead us away from temptation... where you may forget in what country you are travelling; where no farmer can complain that you are treading down his grass... where travellers are not too often to be met; where my spirit is free; where the walls and fences are not cared for, where your head is more in heaven that you feet are on earth; which have long reaches where you can see the approaching traveller half a mile off and be prepared for him... where it makes no odds which way you face, whether you are coming or going... where you can walk and think with least obstruction, there being nothing to measure progress by... There I can walk, and recover the lost child that I am.

HENRY DAVID THOREAU, *A WRITER'S JOURNAL*

Some people are wooed by candlelit dinners,
I am wooed by the open road.

Spud Talbot-Ponsonby

The man who never was lost
never went very far.

G. H. B. Ward, Clarion Handbook, Sheffield Clarion Ramblers
(formed 1900)

Walking, ideally, is a state in which the mind, the body, and the world are aligned...

REBECCA SOLNIT

RESOURCES

WEBSITES:

www.gardendigest.com/walking

www.woodlands.co.uk

www.naturalengland.org.uk

www.walking-routes.co.uk

PUBLICATIONS:

Baker, Margaret *Discovering the Folklore of Plants* (1969, Shire Publications Ltd)

Bardwell, Sandra et al *Walking in Britain (Lonely Planet Walking Guide)* (1997, Lonely Planet Publications)

Country Walking magazine

Johnson, Johnson P. *The Armchair Naturalist: How to be Good at Nature Without Really Trying* (2007, Icon Books Ltd)

Oxford Dictionary of National Biography Series (OUP)

Souter, Gillian *Slow Journeys: The Pleasures of Travelling on Foot* (2009, Allen and Unwin)

Voake, Charlotte *A Little Guide to Wild Flowers* (2007, Eden Project Children's Books)

Walk magazine

ORGANISATIONS:

Ramblers Association
www.ramblers.org.uk

English Heritage
www.english-heritage.org.uk

National Trust
www.nationaltrust.org.uk

Have you enjoyed this book?

If so, why not write a review on your favourite website?

Thanks very much for buying this Summersdale book.

www.summersdale.com